The Diary of a Recycled Dog:

Live, Love, BARK!

The Diary of a Recycled Dog

By

Kim C. Steadman

LIFTER
UPPER
PRESS

THE DIARY OF A RECYCLED DOG

Lifter Upper
PO Box 543211
Grand Prairie, TX 75054
www.LifterUpper.com
To learn more about the author, visit www.KimSteadman.com

Ordering Information:

Quantity sales. Special discounts are available on quantity purchases by corporations, associations, and others. For details, contact the "Special Sales Department" at the address above.

ISBN-13: 978-0-9983419-2-7

ISBN-10:0-9983419-2-4

Contents

For all the throwaway dogs.

Never give up hope.

Live, Love, Bark!

To the kind people at Prairie Paws

Adoption Center, Grand Prairie, TX.

Thank you for all you do.

Introduction:

Unhappy New Year

I don't know how I ended up here. And the people who adopted me will not know either. Yet here I am, and this is my story. The story of how I, an abandoned dog on a dead end road, ended up adopted and loved. Do you want to know what the worst part about it was? It was January 1st. Humans say "Happy New Year" on that day. Well, it wasn't happy for me.

I started my new year frightened and sad. I never talk about my other humans. The ones who abandoned me. I've tried to forget about them. I remember that day and how I saw the taillights of the car as it vanished down the hill. The lights grew smaller in the distance. I hung my head. How could they do this to me?

Surely, my humans didn't leave me here? What are those smells? What are those sounds? I don't like it here. I want to be back at home in my warm bed with my humans. I did not know where they had taken me, and I was afraid. I couldn't see any other humans around. All I could see were trees. I kept thinking, maybe my owners will come back?

When I looked up, the sun had moved across the sky towards the west. By now, the car had completely vanished.

The light of the sun would soon vanish, too. Yet no one had come back for me. Could I find them?

I walked a little way down the road. I will admit to you, I was afraid. The longer my humans stayed away, the more I realized a bad thing had happened. A very bad thing. I was going to be one of them. A throw-away dog. It's every dog's fear. We talk about it in soft, muffled whispers. Abandoned, cast out, and not loved anymore isn't a good thing.

I decided I had to take things into my own paws. I couldn't stay in this spot forever. I needed to find a new home because all dogs want a home. So, I looked to the right. There was nothing but a field and some trees. I looked to my left. It was the road where the car had disappeared. The car that carried my humans far away from me. I guess they're not my humans anymore.

I decided to follow the road. I walked and sniffed. That's when I found the new humans.

Denver's Map

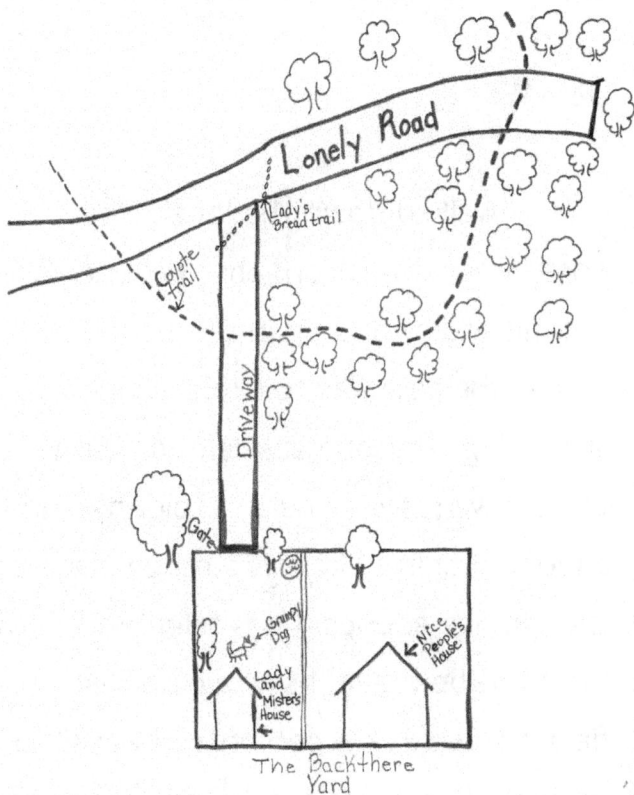

Day 1, Morning:

Bread Trails

Dear World,

I walked down the lonely road. My nose was down on the ground one second and swung up in the air the next. That is the best way to explore when you are a dog. My humans left me alone in this new place where I didn't know anyone. I didn't like this strange place or the strange sounds. I was frightened, but I tried to be brave. I saw a man over in a field. He was a new person, so I was afraid of him. But I decided to put aside my fears and I asked him if he saw the car that left me here. He just walked away.

Then I saw a lady, and I asked her the same questions. "Do you know where my humans went? Have you seen their car?"

She walked away too.

I tried to be brave. I waited a little longer for my owners to return. I sure hoped they would come back for me. I can't believe they left me on purpose. Could it have been an accident? Did someone forget to put me back into the car? But, it had been forever, and they still hadn't come back.

Later, the same lady and man came back. They walked toward me again. Even though I already talked to them before, I was still afraid and started barking. In fear, I wanted to turn back. I wanted to run back down the lonely road to where my owners had left me. But, I knew I couldn't stay there. I knew I needed to find someone I could trust. I also knew I needed to find a new home. But I don't want a new home. I want my old home.

As she walked toward me, I barked some more and wouldn't go over to her. But the lady had a way with animals. She knew the magic of bread for hungry dogs. She took the bread into her hands. The slice was slathered with buttery goodness.

After she broke it into pieces, she placed them on the ground. Then she moved away and gave me some space.

Even though she didn't touch me, she sat on the ground and talked in a soft, kind voice. Her kindness helped me not to feel so afraid.

I ate pieces of food from the ground at first. Then, I put my nose in the air and sniffed. I sat down and thought about this. I could smell more food near her. After some time passed, I moved closer to her. Then, I ate a few pieces near her. She had placed a trail of bread bites leading to a plate next to her.

I followed the bread trail closer to her. After a while, I even ate a few pieces from her hand. I felt as though I could trust her.

She trusted me, too. She put her hand down slowly so I could smell her.

Her fingers smelled like the butter from the bread. I could see some of the melted butter on her fingers, so I licked it.

When I had finished, I didn't have anything to repay her kindness. I didn't have a toy to share with her. I searched for the closest thing I could find, which was a dried tree leaf fluttering across the ground.

I picked it up and brought to her lap. She smiled and talked in a soft voice. When she put her hand out toward me, I stepped back a little bit. But, she kept whispering to me. Then she placed her hand on the ground for me to sniff.

Soon, I moved closer and put my head on her hand. Her fingers found my favorite spot under my chin. I knew this was someone who would help me. I decided to call her Lady.

I wagged my curly tail at her. She laughed quietly, and that made my tail wag even harder.

She laughed some more and then said, "Dog, we need to get you off the road to somewhere safe."

She carefully got up from where she sat on the ground. I followed her, and soon we walked onto a little rocky road. She explained we had to go this way to get to the house where she and the man lived.

There were lots of new smells along the way. I smelled something and started following the trail.

Lady said, "Dog, you smell coyotes. It is the trail they usually follow when they pass through this property. Then they go up toward the end of the street where you were. You want to stay far away from them. They are dangerous to little dogs."

Denver's Dog Wisdom:
Follow your nose.

Day 1, Evening:

Rescued

We finally made it to a fenced yard. Lady opened the gate and walked in. Then she invited me into the yard. I could hear a muffled bark coming from inside the house. I wasn't too sure about this new place. Cautiously, I took a few small steps as I walked slowly through the gate. I needed to be alert in case I needed to make a quick escape.

The man greeted me with a soft voice. "Hi, there Dog. You're a cute little fellow." I decided to call him Mister.

I was glad he spoke in a kind voice to me. I soaked in several new smells and sounds. My sniffer went into overdrive at this point, as I ran around the yard so my nose could touch each and every smell. The lady said, "Dog, you smell squirrels, raccoons, opossums, and another little dog." I didn't know what some of those things were. But I could hear that little dog barking. He sounded small and yappy.

Lady and Mister looked at me. I didn't have a collar. Then Lady lifted my brown floppy ears to look inside for a tattoo of ownership. It tickled and I shook my head. Finally, she put me down on the ground and I was ready to play. But instead of letting me play, she went into the house.

She brought out a pink harness for me to wear.

"Sorry little guy, but this harness used to belong to our old cat. She crossed the rainbow bridge a few months ago. I couldn't find it in my heart to part with it. It's a good thing I kept it because it looks like it will fit you," said Lady.

And she was right! The harness did fit me. Lady didn't think I was used to wearing one. But, she told me I was a good dog for adapting so quickly.

Finally, it was time to play and explore some more. After I played in the yard with leaves, sticks, and an old ball, Lady said, "Dog, you need to meet someone." She opened the front door while Mister held me. Out rushed the little yapping dog. He was black, but his head and muzzle were full of gray hairs. I could tell he was old.

By the sounds of his yelling, he was also grumpy. Since I didn't know how long I would be at this house, I knew I needed to be careful not to make him mad.

"Let me tell you something!" he yelled. "I've been the top dog here on this hill for a very long time. And I'm not used to visitors. I'm grumpy, and this is my space!"

I decided that from now on, and unless things changed, I would call him Grumpy Dog. Grumpy Dog's introduction wasn't quite the welcome I wanted. But, what choice did I have? I knew I didn't want to go back to the lonely road. Besides, I liked Lady and Mister. I decided I would be careful to give Grumpy Dog his space.

When the sun dipped below the trees, Lady said we needed to go into the house.

"What are we going to do with Dog?" asked Mister.

Lady told him to wait a minute, and she went into the house. Soon, she came back outside carrying something. It was a leash.

They kept me on a leash inside the house and let me walk around and explore things. Grumpy Dog gargled at me as he gave me a sideways glance. But

Lady ignored him and kept a firm hand on my leash. Grumpy Dog and I went nose to rump a couple of times and sniffed each other. Yet he didn't snap at me, and I was glad for that.

I understood the look he gave me without him saying a thing. He planted his paws on the ground as if to say, "This is my turf. Keep your distance." But he didn't have to worry about that. I'm a smart dog. Still, my tail wagged at him because I wanted to play with him.

Later in the evening, we settled down to watch TV. The man invited me up onto his lap. I liked that. My eyelids grew heavy the longer I sat still. I fell asleep, and Lady later told me that I had sighed deeply. I guess I knew I was in a safe place for the evening.

I woke up a little later and licked Mister's face.

"Hey, Dog, would you like to go outside?" Mister asked.

They took me outside, and I went potty.

"You are a good dog!" exclaimed Lady.

I liked the sound of those words —"good dog"—so I wagged my tail at her. I don't know why she laughed every time I wagged my tail. It's curly, but when it moved, it flopped over from side to side. I guess that's what made her laugh.

The evening went on, and it came time for bed. The people hadn't been prepared to take in a 12 pound, young boy like me. They decided that the man would sleep in his chair with me and the lady would sleep in bed with Grumpy Dog. As I settled into Mister's lap, I determined that nice people rescued me.

Denver's Dog Wisdom:
Be willing to make new friends.

Day 2, Morning:

A New World

Dear World,

Last night was long. I was a little nervous in my new surroundings, and I woke up about every two hours. Mister took me out for potty breaks whenever I stirred. He was patient and spoke kindly to me. I sure was thankful because this was a new world for me.

The morning sun barely shined in through the window when I heard a noise that woke me up. Someone was walking in the hallway. As they peeked their head around the corner, I let out a bark. I tried to warn Mister. But, then I saw it was Lady.

She said, "Dog, Grumpy Dog needs to go potty. Would you like to go outside too?"

I decided that was a good idea. So I went outside and did my business. Lady smiled and told me I was a good boy. I liked that.

Then, Lady asked Mister how I did through the night. I looked up at him and tilted my head. He looked a little worn out. I don't suppose he was used to sleeping in a chair all night or taking potty breaks every two hours. But, he told Lady things went well.

Seeing that Lady could take care of the dogs on her own, he went to bed to catch up on his sleep. Lady watched over me during the morning hours.

Later, I wanted to play outside, but it was raining. Grumpy Dog looked frightened. Lady sat in her chair and held him.

Lady explained Grumpy Dog's reaction. "He gets scared during rainstorms, Dog. I have to hold him in my arms. Then I walk him around the house to settle him down. Or, I hold him in my lap."

But, I didn't mind the thunder. Even though I wasn't afraid, she still invited me to sit in her lap with Grumpy Dog.

He did not enjoy my presence in her lap, but he didn't yell at me either. I decided not to take any chances. So I moved as far to the other side of the chair as I could without falling off. I thought Lady seemed a little bit tired, too. We all must have been tired. Soon, all three of us fell asleep again.

Later, we sat in the house, and watched the rain. She took my picture.

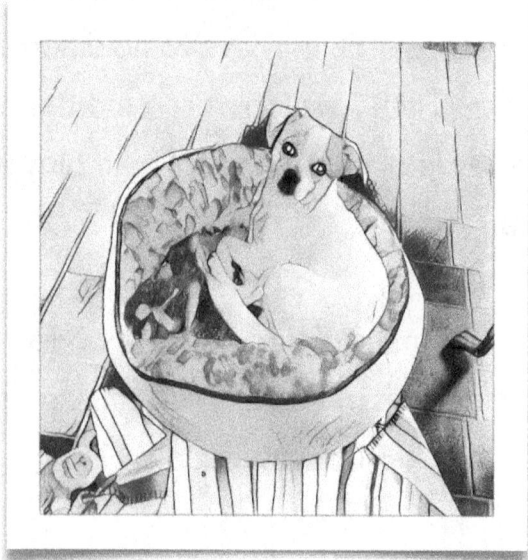

"Dog, if you are lost, we need to try to find your owners."

I wanted to tell her that I wasn't lost. She made some phone calls to try to find my home. Lady and Mister started talking about what to call me.

Mister said, "I would like to call him something besides Dog while he is here."

They talked about different names, and I listened to them. They would say a name while looking at me, hoping it sounded familiar. But, none of them did.

Finally, Lady said, "Let's call him Denver. His fur is white like the snow on the mountains in Colorado."

So that's how I got the name, Denver. I liked the name. I wagged my tail to let them know having a name made me feel special.

Truthfully, I didn't know what my future held. But I was just glad I had a warm, safe place to stay.

Denver's Dog Wisdom:
Don't let bad things from yesterday spoil your fun today.

Day 2, Evening:

Take a Little Trip

Dear World,

In the afternoon, the sun came out, and the rain stopped. Lady let me play outside for a little while even though it was muddy. I wanted to play in the yard, but I didn't want my paws to get wet. So I stayed on the porch. I sure wished I had a chew stick or something.

Lady sat in her rocking chair on the porch. I sniffed at her house shoes. Lady said I couldn't chew on her house shoes, so I stopped. How did she know I even thought about it?

Lady and Mister planned to foster me until they could find me a home. But before they made any promises, they wanted to make sure I was healthy enough to be around their little dog. So they arranged a trip to the vet.

I walked on the leash and out the gate. But, when Lady got close to the car, I dug my paws into the ground to keep from going near the big machine.

Despite my protests, they put me in the car anyway. I won't lie to you. I was not happy about the car ride. I had bad memories of cars. I shook like a leaf in the wind. Lady cradled me in her lap while Mister drove the car.

The vet needed to test my stool sample, which Lady already had. She gave it to them in a little bag.

After testing it, the girl came back and said, "He's negative." She smiled as she spoke.

Her smile made me feel better. She then explained to me that negative was good. I'm glad because negative sounded bad to me.

Mister asked, "How old do you think he is? What type of dog is he?"

I looked up at him and tilted my head. "I am a good dog," I tried to tell him. "Is there any other kind?"

She thought I was not even two years old yet and said that I weighed 13 pounds. "Overall, he appears to be healthy," she said.

When it was time to get back into the car, I shivered and shook. Seriously, I don't like cars now. I wasn't sure about the ride at first, but I settled into Lady's lap.

They decided to take me to a store for pet supplies to find a chewy toy for me.

Lady said, "It's time to go to a fun place. Not all car rides are bad!"

When we arrived at the pet store, Lady carried me inside and then put me down on the floor. I had on the pink harness and a leash. As I took one step forward I wondered, Is this dog heaven? I could smell so many smells.

She let me walk around and I didn't tug on the leash. Oops. I tugged on the leash near the bags of food. Who decided to put bags of food so low to the ground in a store like this? One bag, called "cat food," smelled really good and I gnawed on the corner. But, Lady heard me and made me stop.

This store was full of good smells and toys. I felt so happy when we were there. I even met a little friend who was on a leash too! We talked about what we ate for breakfast before Lady dragged me along.

As we walked by, a woman exclaimed, "He is very cute!"

Lady and Mister told her my story. Then, the woman said she would take me home. But Lady said someone else might want me, too.

The woman said, "Remember me if you need a home for him! I'll take him!"

That made two possible new homes for me!

After the shopping visit, I decided that all car rides are not bad.

One of the things Lady and Mister loaded into the car was a kennel.

"You'll need a safe place to sleep at night or when we leave the house, Denver," said Lady. She didn't know what I would think about it.

Later that afternoon, Lady set up the kennel. Then, she opened a cheese stick. When she unwrapped the crinkly cheese wrapper, my head tilted to the side. My curly tail wagged and I pranced a happy step.

"You recognize that sound, don't you, Boy?" She smiled at me.

I watched carefully as she placed two bites inside. Lady said the word "kennel" and pointed to the inside of the kennel where the cheese was. I surprised her when I went inside after a tiny, little nudge. We did this exercise a couple of times. The last time, she closed the door. Then she walked out of the room. I tried to be good. I didn't cry or bark.

She came back quickly, let me out, and exclaimed, "Denver, you are a good dog!"

Next, Lady took some little dog biscuits and put them in the cage. I went inside and grabbed them real fast and ate them outside. Fool me once, shame on you. Fool me twice, shame on me I thought to myself.

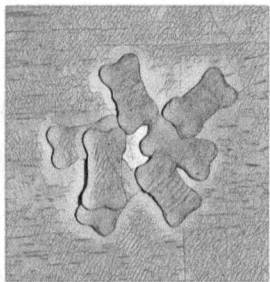

She put two more little dog biscuits into the kennel and then walked away. She said, "I want your kennel to be your happy place."

Later, she puttered around the kitchen. Those biscuits called my name. I went inside the kennel to eat them and decided the kennel wasn't a bad place. So I curled up and took a little nap. The last thing I saw before my eyes closed were smiles on Lady and Mister's faces. I think I made them happy.

When I woke up, we played outside. Mister and Lady said it was going to get cold later this week so we had to take advantage of the nice weather. I found a sunny place on the porch. The sunbeam felt good, and I felt happy and safe.

When we came inside, Lady fed Grumpy Dog and me. She had our bowls on opposite sides of the room.

Grumpy said, "I don't like company when I eat."

But we ate at the same time, in the same room, so that meant we ate together, right? All I knew was it felt good to have a full belly.

While we ate, Lady cooked food for her and Mister. I liked the smells when she cooked.

"Have you noticed he did not beg when I cooked?" she asked as they sat down to eat. "He didn't cause any trouble."

I surprised her again and went inside the kennel on my own. As I lay down to take a nap, I decided it was not a bad place, really. I scratched on the fluffy pad and curled up. The last thing I saw before my eyelids closed was Lady and Mister smiling.

During the evening Mister and Lady sat in their chairs, and my eyelids became heavy. I fell asleep in Mister's lap. They giggled when I started to snore.

Later, Lady said, "You know what, Grumpy Dog only growled at Denver when they ate. And Denver did not say anything back to him."

I'm a smart dog. I've learned to let him go out the door first when we go potty. He likes to be first. And I let him have his space when he eats.

Lady said it was her turn to sleep in the chair with me. Oh, good, I thought. That meant I didn't have to sleep in the kennel.

Denver's Dog Wisdom:
Don't bite or growl at old dogs.

Day 3:

New Routines

Dear World,

It was a different day today. Mister left the house early in the morning. Lady said he went to a place called work. I did not like it when he left. So I sat in the hallway and stared at the door for a little while. Then, she said that today I had to do some homework.

I practiced "sit" and "kennel up." I did not really like kennel up. What made it even worse was that Lady left the room the first time we practiced. But, the second time, she went out the back door and was gone for two whole minutes. Those two minutes seemed like forever. I was so glad when she came back.

After homework time inside, we played in the yard. It was cold with lots of wind. I did not like the wind, although I

did like how the wind blew my leaves around. I barked at the leaves as they flew past me. Lady said I have a big bark even though I'm a little guy. I also played with my other favorite thing in the whole wide world—sticks!

Since Lady slept in the chair with me last night, she was a little tired today.

In the afternoon, she said, "Boys, I need a nap."

Lady finally listened to Grumpy Dog and me. We had both wanted to take a nap. She sat in her chair and invited us both to sit with her. Grumpy Dog only fussed a little bit when I got into her lap. We all fell asleep quickly.

When I awoke, something wonderful happened. Mister finally came home! I romped and ran because I was so excited to see him. He rubbed my belly, and it felt good.

After he finished petting me, Lady fed Grumpy Dog and me. He only growled at me once. But, that was my fault. I forgot my limits and got a little too close.

When we ran outside after dinner, we got close together because of all the excitement. What was the excitement? Raccoons were at the gate!

Lady said they were okay and told us not bark at them. But, Grumpy Dog told me otherwise.

"Bark at them, Whippersnapper! That lets them know they are in our territory. You want to make sure they know this is our yard!" Grumpy exclaimed loudly.

He didn't have to tell me twice! I fell in line behind Grumpy Dog and barked at them, too!

I had never seen raccoons before. They were a furry gray ball of fluff with a mask across their eyes. Grumpy Dog and I had fun running along the fence line, casing after them.

After we came inside I realized something. He called me Whippersnapper! He didn't growl at me! He talked to me! Lady explained the long, strange name. "Whippersnapper is sometimes what old people call young kids." I did not care what he called me. I liked that he had a name for me.

Evening finally came, and it was time for Mister to sit in his chair. As soon as he plopped into the fluffy chair, I jumped up in his lap. I've decided I like this routine. He must like it too because he smiled at me.

Later, Lady announced, "It's time for bed!"

But, this time, instead of finding a comfy chair like we did the last two nights, Lady went to the kennel. Oh, no! Not the kennel.

Mister said, "Let's see how he does sleeping in our bedroom."

I was not sure what was about to happen. I had not been in that room, yet.

But it had to be better than being on my own.

Lady lifted my kennel and moved it into their bedroom. She placed it on the floor on her side of the bed. Then, she opened the door and knelt in front of it. I peeked around the corner of the bed. Then I surprised Lady. I went into the kennel by myself! She didn't even have to give me a nudge or a push.

"What a good dog you are, Denver!"

She gave me several belly rubs and softly said these words to me. "Denver, you are a good dog. You are a smart dog. You are a special dog."

You know what? I've decided I am a good dog! Lady and Mister helped me to see I'm not a throwaway dog!

Denver's Dog Wisdom:
Don't judge an old dog by his gray hairs. They have a friendly side, you just need to find it.

Day 4:

Lost dog

Dear World,

I had a fun day of playing. I also met the people next door. When we got there, Grumpy Dog let me know there was a special pillow I was not supposed to touch. In fact, he didn't even want me to look that direction.

"That is my pillow you little Whippersnapper. Stay far away from it," he said.

That's ok because there were a lot of new smells I needed to investigate.

When we got home Lady helped me practice "kennel up." I stayed for a LONG time! Five minutes was FOREVER in dog time. When she returned and let me out of the kennel, I ran to the door to go potty. That made her smile real big, and she said, "Good boy, Denver!"

But her smile was not big when I went pee-pee in the house later in the day. I tried to tell her to open the door faster, but she didn't listen. She said she would listen next time.

Lady and Mister decided they wanted to do the right thing to make sure someone could adopt me. They took me to a place where a lady with a nice voice scanned my back to see if I had a chip. Even though she had a nice voice, I did not like what she did to me. But I didn't growl or whimper. I just wiggled.

A chip is how lost pets and owners can be reunited. Since I did not have one, it meant they could not contact my old owners. I'm glad they can't be found. They abandoned me, so I don't want to go back to them.

Lady and Mister were sad when they realized that someone abandoned me. I heard Mister and Lady say the words "we will take care of him." They talked with the people at the shelter about my future.

One lady took my picture. Another lady gave me a shot and I wiggled some more. Then she put yucky stuff in my nose. I wiggled and jiggled this time. They said it was to make sure I stay healthy. Staying healthy sometimes means doing yucky things. I did not like it. But I never growled or whimpered.

The lady at the shelter said Lady and Mister needed to wait 72 hours.

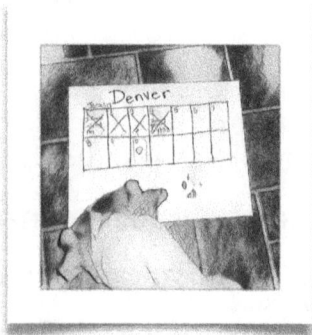

That's three whole days. After the waiting was over, someone could adopt me. Since it was the weekend, she said it would be longer. Mister and Lady said it was okay and they did not mind if I stayed with them.

Mister and Lady also told them they would be the ones to find me a forever home. I didn't know what a forever home was but I liked the sound of it.

Mister said, "Someone will have to answer lots of questions and show lots of proof before they can have him."

I felt like a criminal because they said I had a booking number. The people entered me into the computer system. To the animal shelter, I was booking number A149518.

But Lady and Mister said, "Don't worry. To us, your name is Denver."

One of the nice people at the shelter said it was a good thing they found me. But I thought it was a good thing I found them.

When we got into the car, Lady said I was a good dog. She gave me lots of rubs and pats on my head. While she softly stroked my fur, I fell asleep as we drove home. It was not a long drive, but this was a lot of excitement for a dog like me!

Denver's Dog Wisdom:
Pee-Pee, Poop, Doodle or whatever you call it. Do it outside and you get smiles, but in the house you get frowns.

Day 5:

New Friends

Dear World,

I slept like a rock last night! I woke up to some colder weather though. When I went outside, the wind started blowing and cold air blew my ears! I sure was glad I found Lady and Mister. If I had survived the first four days by dodging wild coyotes, I'm not sure how I would have survived this cold air.

I did not like the wind when it blew my ears. But, I did like the wind when it moved the leaves. Every time Lady let me outside to go potty, I chased the leaves.

I also brought in a stick. But, Lady did not let me keep it.

"Denver, there are no sticks allowed in the house. That's the rule. They aren't good for you to chew," she explained.

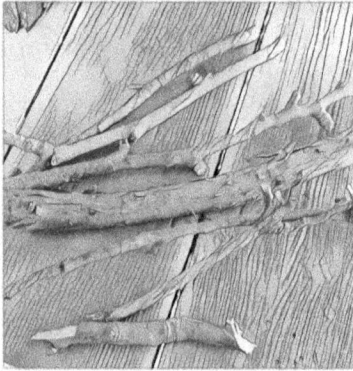

I did not like that rule. I tried to bring in a stick every time she let me outside. But she kept telling me "No." So I switched to something else. Something just as fun!

I decided to bring leaves in instead. She tried to take those away, too. But, I nibbled some of them. She said I was silly and told me to stop acting like a squirrel or a rabbit. But, she said it with a smile on her face, so I knew she wasn't mad.

Lady said it was time to visit the neighbors. They must be really nice people because when Lady said their names, Grumpy Dog bounced up and down and wagged his little tail. I didn't know that little, old guy had that much bounce in him. He was so excited he even let me stand next to him at the door while we waited to go outside.

Lady put the leash on my harness and led me next door.

She carefully opened the door and said, "You have a visitor."

I was a good boy while we were there. Lady kept me on the leash as I walked around the new house. I explored many new smells, but I also smelled familiar smells like Grumpy Dog and Lady.

After we got back home Lady said it was time to do homework. I was happy and ready to learn. Grumpy Dog decided he wanted in on the action. He sat by her while she taught me.

Lady was proud of me when I did 'kennel up.' I didn't go in willingly. But, she put me in, and I didn't whimper. Then, she went outside to do something. It seemed like she was gone forever. But, she said it was only 10 minutes. When she let me out, I ran around the house like a dog chasing a cat (of course I would NEVER chase a cat). She laughed. I liked to hear Lady laugh.

Lady gave me pats and treats, and she commanded me to "sit." Then, Grumpy Dog decided he wanted treats so he sat down too. I decided I would sit again without being asked. I thought if I hunkered my bottom down harder and faster than the last time, she would make the bits of treats even bigger.

She didn't. Oh well, it was worth a try.

Mister came home from work, and I was so happy to see him. Lady laughed at how much my tail wagged and how it flopped loosely from one side to the other. I think it's a good wag. They understood my message. I was happy. I rested in my favorite patch of grass.

I overheard Lady and Mister talking. They said they couldn't understand how someone could have abandoned me. Lady's eyes were misty as she held back her tears. She said it wasn't fair because they didn't even give me a chance to find new people. They dumped me at the end of a road.

That was all she said. She had to stop talking because she was so upset. Mister said maybe I was an angel dog sent to them for a special reason. I liked the thought of being an angel dog.

She told Mister that whatever made my owners dislike me was in the past. She said that each day was new and I would have a second chance with a brand new family. Then they told me special news.

"Denver, we have decided to make you part of our family."

Lady knelt down on the floor with Grumpy dog and me and she gave us belly rubs. Grumpy Dog never growled at me. He didn't smile, but he didn't growl. Maybe he has started to like me a little more. I sure hope so.

Denver's Dog Wisdom:
Good things come when you don't expect it.

Day 6:

New Weather

Dear World,

Could this day have started any better? I don't think so. Grumpy Dog and I started the morning by chasing an intruder out of the front yard! It was early morning and the sun had barely come up over the trees. I learned that these strange creatures liked to sneak over the fence and into the yard. Lady and Mister had a fountain in the corner for the birds. But, the raccoons drank from there, too.

To reach the fountain, they balanced on the fence as they made their way across.

Grumpy Dog told me, "Whippersnapper, never miss an opportunity to bark at the raccoons. They run and scramble. If you are lucky, they run up into the tree and then stare at you. You can bark at them until Lady tells you to be quiet."

They did not run up the tree. But I liked chasing them as they scrambled over the fence. But Lady said that we need to be kind to them. Truthfully, I don't know what I would do if I were to catch one. I think I will stick to the advice Grumpy gave me and stay far enough behind them since they are almost as big as me.

Today was one of those days that Mister didn't have to go to work. He spent time with me outside and I showed him how I could collect leaves and sticks. Those were my favorite things to hunt for in the yard. But, I didn't get to hunt for long. It was cold outside and things seemed different.

Later, I realized what was so different.

Lady announced, "It's snowing outside guys!" She opened the door and Grumpy Dog and I ran outside to have a look.

I don't know why she said it with such gladness in her voice. We learned quickly snow meant a cold ground and cold air! Grumpy Dog and I decided to take fast potty breaks because it chilled us to the bone.

Snow fell almost all day. The light fluffy flakes covered the ground. Because we were stuck inside all day, Lady and Mister learned how young and active I was.

"You are a bundle of energy, Denver." said Lady.

Since it was cold and wet outside, I couldn't play out there. It ended up being a long day of playing chase indoors and laying by the fireplace. Since there weren't any leaves and sticks to hunt, Lady and Mister took turns tossing toys for me so I could run and fetch them.

I'm sure glad Lady and Mister were patient with me. It's hard to stay calm when being trapped indoors.

When we played, Lady noticed something special about my fur. "Denver, some of the spots on your back are shaped like hearts." Sure enough, they found three hearts on my back.

"You have love on the inside and love on the outside!" she said as she gave me belly rubs.

When it was time for bed, we went through our usual routine. After five days, I already knew what "bedtime" meant. I waited for her to put my kennel next to the bed. Don't get me wrong; I didn't prance into it like a circus dog. But, with her gentle voice, she told me how smart and good I was. Then, she gave me belly rubs, and soon, I curled up inside snug, happy, and sleepy.

Denver's Dog Wisdom:
Be willing to listen to the older dogs. Sometimes they know fun stuff.

Day 7:

White Stuff Go Away

Dear World,

Today, Lady said, "Denver, we will have to do all our playing inside."

That is not the news I wanted to hear. I was thankful for being warm and safe in this house with Mister, Lady, and Grumpy Dog. But, I really did like to play outside. Yet I knew that I couldn't go outside in this weather. I'm a little guy and my fur is short and slick. The weather made me shiver yesterday so I knew I would shiver more today.

Grumpy Dog and I decided we didn't like snow. He didn't like it because he's so short.

"I don't have long legs like you, Whippersnapper. My belly rides low and I get cold on the bottom and on the top."

He was right about that. I am a little bit taller than he is.

But besides the chill on our paws, bellies, and back, the snow hid things. It hid my leaves and my sticks. I tried to nose around to get one. The snow wasn't deep enough to completely cover them. I could see the leaves poking through a little bit. When I snatched one with my teeth, the cold snow flew up onto my face.

I had several quick potty breaks throughout the day. Even if I didn't need to go outside to potty, I stood in the hallway. I stared at the door and hoped that when it opened, there would be sun. I missed the sun.

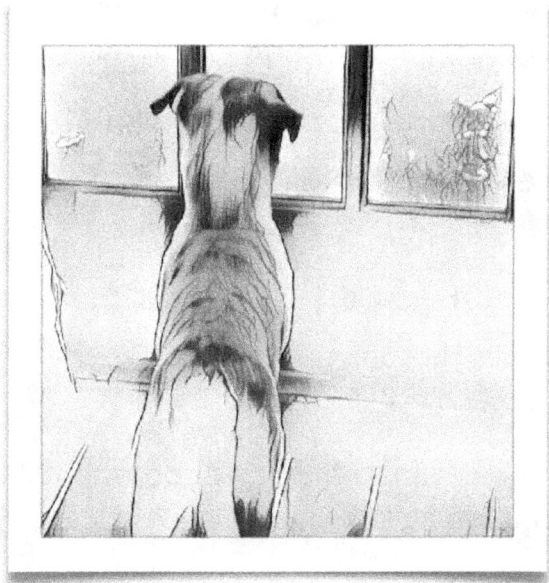

But more snow fluttered and fell. Mister went to the door several times to check the weather. I had hoped he would make it stop or go away, but he did not. I had to be satisfied playing inside. I sure was glad Lady was so patient with me.

Later in the day, I sat at Mister's feet while he cleaned his desk. Suddenly, I saw something move. There was a masked intruder so close to the backdoor I could smell him! I started yelling at Mister.

He said, "Denver, it's only one those raccoons.

I ran to the other room to tell Lady that we had a visitor. "He's here! He's here!" I exclaimed to her.

Lady said it was okay. "He can stay there, Denver. He will not hurt anything."

She told me to stop barking. But I tried to convince her to let me go outside and chase him. She said no. "He's back there in the back yard where the field meets the yard. Little dogs can't go back there." My ears drooped a little. I can see The Back There Yard. It looked like a fun place to explore.

But I perked up when I realized that I had an important job to do. My task for the evening was to patrol the back door and make sure the intruder didn't come back. I must have done a good job because I did not see him again.

Later that evening, Lady crawled on the floor and played with me. The big shock was that Grumpy Dog started to play us. He was on the love seat and started making weird, grunting sounds.

Lady said, "Denver, he's trying to play with you. Be gentle, because he's so small."

He then let out a playful bark. I didn't know that sound could come out of his mouth because all I've heard were his little growls. I tilted my head to listen some more. His tail even wagged! Did that mean he liked me?

I was so excited and happy, I told him how I felt. I think I spoke too loudly though. It scared him a little bit. But, that small amount of playtime gave me hope.

Maybe Grumpy Dog would be my friend after all.

When we went to bed, I gave Lady a surprise. I walked into my kennel without needing a treat or needing a push. I was tired. She was so happy! She gave me lots of belly rubs and told me what a good dog I was and how I was smart. I guess the snow and cold air made me extra tired because I drifted off to sleep immediately.

Denver's Dog Wisdom:
Good things happen when you least expect them.

Day 8:

New Discoveries

Dear World,

"I am a good dog. I am a special boy." Those were the words I dreamed about last night. It made my tail wag while I slept. Today was my One Week Finding Them Birthday. It had been the happiest week of my life. I even gave Lady a special treat when I slept for eight whole hours!

Today I practiced commands with Lady for a little bit. She got very excited when I obeyed. She gave me lots of belly rubs. When she said "down" and pointed to the ground, I went down onto my belly. She didn't think I listened yesterday when she taught me this, but I did! I also learned "jump" and jumped up into her arms.

Morning went by as usual, and then it happened. Lady said "kennel up" and I was such a good boy and went inside with no help (well, almost no help). Then, Lady and Mister both left the house. Wait! I thought. I did not like the idea of both people leaving at the same time. They said they were going to church and would be leaving the house for a while. That was not what I had expected. And exactly how long was a while? I didn't like the sound of that.

I waited. And waited. I waited for what seemed like forever. Grumpy Dog did a little walk through and passed by my kennel. I tried to ignore the smug look on his face. It was fine that he was out there. At least, that's what I tried to tell myself.

After all, I still had treats in my kennel. But I decided I wouldn't eat them just yet. I thought I might need them if I started to starve. *How long would Lady and Mister be gone?*

To pass the time, I played with my chewy. I flipped it up, and it landed outside the bars of the kennel, rolling onto my blanket. I tried to pull my blanket inside the crate. At least tugging on the blanket kept me busy while I waited. And waited. And I waited some more.

Finally, I heard the familiar rattle of the doorknob as Lady and Mister opened the front door. They were finally home!

They let me outside to potty. But, I ran around and barked. I tried to tell them I didn't like how long they left me alone. I also told them I was a good boy! I figured out that I could wait and I would not starve.

Today I also learned about the squeak. It's a secret thing put into the center of some dog and cat toys. One of my favorite toys I've been playing with is shaped like a mouse. It must have belonged to the old cat. It fit perfectly in my mouth.

Lady thought it was funny when I put the toy into my mouth in just the right position I could squeeze my jaw and it would squeak. And squeak. And squeak. And squeak. I could have gone on like that for hours! This mouse toy had the best squeak of them all.

Lady said, "Denver if you capture the squeaker, it will not make the fun noise anymore." I thought about it for a minute. I decided it was worth it so I chewed more.

Later, Mister watched a football game on TV, and I curled up in his lap and slept. I was very thankful they didn't leave me alone on that deserted road. They took a chance on me when they invited me into their home.

When it was time for bed, Lady led me to the kennel. Once I was inside she softly rubbed my belly and repeated my special words. "Denver, you are a good dog. You are a smart dog and you are a special dog."

Denver's Dog Wisdom:
Use your imagination and make your own fun.

Day 9:

New Surprises

Dear World,

It's official. I was not fond of the wind. This blustery day disturbed my usual joy for the magic word "outside."

The first problem was that there were too many leaves blowing around. Remember though, I like leaves. No, I love leaves. Lady said I was obsessed with them. Every time I went outside, I pounced on a leaf and tried to bring it inside. I had to run past Lady and eat it before she snatched it away.

Today, the wind blew the leaves at me like a raging bunch of wild animals. It was them against little me. I am 13 pounds of sturdy spunkiness, but I had my limits. I barked at Lady to warn her.

They swirled around on the other side of

the gate. I thought they were going to come in and get me!

Lady let me play outside for a long time. I surprised Lady when I ran from the water hose. She filled the birdbaths, and I ran away from the water sloshing. She thought I was afraid of the water. Maybe I am frightened, or maybe I wanted her to think I was scared. I knew that water equals baths. And I don't like baths.

Today, Grumpy Dog and I stunned Lady. Lady was on the floor with both of us. She rubbed our bellies and talked in her sweet, baby talk voice to us.

She said, "I speak in baby voices, so Grumpy Dog will continue to learn to like you, Denver."

When she used her baby voice, he forgot I was near. We lay close together while she gave us belly rubs.

She tried to fold the laundry today, but I tugged at some of the towels and blankets.   She smiled and said, "Your mouth may get you into trouble."

I tilted my head, perked up my ears and gave her my cute look. Was she right? She smiled at me so I was not in trouble, yet.

Grumpy Dog and I practiced our homework again. Lady looked at me and told me to sit. You know what happened next? Grumpy Dog sat with me! She then said "down' and pointed toward the ground. Grumpy Dog and I did down, together! We were like a circus act! It made Lady happy, and she laughed. She gave us many more belly rubs. We did it together two more times. She said we were both beautiful, smart dogs.

I told Grumpy Dog, "Hang around with me Old-timer, and I will teach you some manners."

Grumpy Dog reminded me who had to sit in "kennel up" during church yesterday. Oh well. I guess we both need to learn a few things.

The wind finally stopped howling when it was almost time for bed. I was glad. Grumpy dog and I went outside for our nightly potty. I chased the leaves, and they didn't chase me.

Lady said it was time for bed. I walked inside the crate and waited for her special words. I loved hearing her gentle voice and my special words before going to sleep.

"Denver, you are a good dog. You are a smart dog. You are a special dog." said Lady. I was content, sighed and went to sleep.

Denver's Dog Wisdom:
It's fun to do things with friends.

Day 10:

A New Family

Dear World,

Today was the day! Lady signed my dog adoption papers. She went to the city animal services and claimed me.

Even though it was such an important day, I still had tasks to do. My job was to find the leaves, catch the leaves, and then shred them into tiny pieces. Those dead leaves won't blow around and chase me again.

It was such a sunny and warm day; I had plenty of leaf hunting time. Oh, and sticks. I searched for sticks, too. But, Lady wouldn't let me chew on those if she saw me. She took them away and then put a chewy in my mouth. She didn't seem to understand that those sticks tasted much better.

We spent the afternoon outside. I was tired and decided to take a nap. Maybe it was because I was actually part of the family now, but Grumpy Dog finally lay down beside me. That made Lady smile.

After Mister came home from work, he set up a strange surprise. He took the cover off a huge contraption. It scared me at first. But I got over that quickly when I saw Lady carry a plate and hand it to Mister. He put something inside that thing. Later the smells made me tilt my nose up high in the air. Then he carried those good smells into the house. I didn't even care about going outside anymore. Leaf catching was no longer important!

But I didn't get any of those good smells in my dinner bowl. The funny thing was, Grumpy Dog didn't either. He cast me a sideways glance as if to say he used to get a bite or two of those good smells. Hamburgers were what Lady called them.

Let me tell you, he wasn't too happy about missing out on that treat.

"Thanks to you Whippersnapper, I didn't get a bite of hamburger." He plopped on his bottom and ate his kibble. But he looked at Lady and whined.

I curled up on my blanket and took a nap while they ate. I noticed Grumpy Dog quit whining, and later, he pranced by with a smug look on his face. I wonder if Lady gave him a little bite? He sure seemed satisfied. Oh, well. That's okay.

He's old, cranky and needs special attention sometimes.

Denver's Dog Wisdom:
You don't need all the attention all of the time. Share your people and share your food.

Day 11:

A New Tomorrow

Dear World,

When it was finally time for bed, Lady let us outside for our bed-time potty. That's when all the action started. The masked intruder was in the yard again. Grumpy Dog and I were excited. Our tails wagged, and we ran around the yard. Once we finally sent him the message to go away, Lady said it was time to go inside. I didn't want to go in though. I dragged my paws into the house.

We went to the bedroom to get ready for bed. Lady folded a blanket, or at least she tried to. I tugged at the corners.

"You know, Denver, your mouth may get you into trouble."

I tilted my head, perked up my ears and gave her my cute look. She may be right.

"Alright guys, now it's time to go to sleep," Lady said, with a tired sigh.

But I still didn't want to. It was the first time I was stubborn about going to bed. Lady and Mister didn't understand that I still had a big job to do. I needed to catch more leaves, and someone needed to watch for the masked intruder.

Lady had to nudge me twice to go into the kennel. I sighed, scratched a spot on the mat, turned in circles, and curled up. I dreamed about chasing leaves until Grumpy Dog woke us up in the middle of the night. He had an upset stomach.

I couldn't help but chuckle to myself as I followed them outside. *That's what he got for eating a bite of hamburger.*

He spent lots of time roaming in the grass and chewing off bits of grass to settle his stomach. I played in the grass while Lady sat on the porch. We waited for him to feel better. Guess what happened next? I'll tell you! The masked intruder came back into the yard! We tried to tell everyone.

Lady shushed us and said, "You two are making a ruckus."

Oh well. The intruder left so that meant we did our job. Of course, we had to do a quick patrol of the fence line to make sure he didn't sneak back over.

As we walked back into the house, Lady said it was going to be a long day. Good, that meant I would have more time for leaf catching! It was too late to go back to bed because Mister would be up soon. So we all sat in the comfy chair while Lady read.

After Mister had left for work, Lady said, "Denver, we are your forever family now. I better make this house more Denver-proof." She spent the rest of the day rearranging cords, shoes, pillows, blankets, and curtains. "It's like having a baby in the house. You like to chew things."

I do love to chew. But I was glad I had my chew toys so I didn't get in trouble for nibbling on something I was not supposed to. I was also thankful that

Lady was smart and wanted to help me to not be tempted.

Denver's Dog Wisdom:
Family is anyone who loves all of you, even your flaws.

Denver Explores

The happy week ended by meeting some special people. They had a little person in their family and I got to meet him. Lady thought I would like to play with him, and she was right.

But she gave me a warning before letting me go play. "Denver, he's a little guy and I don't want you to be too rough. Remember to be gentle. Just like you have to be with old, Grumpy Dog."

I was very glad to meet him! My tail wagged and he laughed. We spent the day playing outside. He even purposely dropped some food on the floor so I could eat it. I was sure we would be good buddies.

My story doesn't end here, but these were the most exciting times of my new new life. I met some great people who restored my faith in humans. Even though I was abandoned I was found, and then finally loved. I was given a second chance at life and I have never been happier.

Lady reminds me often, "One person's trash is another person's treasure. Denver, you are our treasure."

I have many more adventures to share as I discover the new sights, sounds, and places with my new humans. You and your grown-ups can find out about my new books and adventures at www.DenverTheDog.com.

Tell your grown-ups about my new dog joke book coming soon!

Stray Animal Safety

The Humane Society has provided some helpful tips kids and their grown-ups for what to do if you see a stray dog.

For the Kids:

- Never approach an animal you do not know. Animals in vehicles and yards may guard their territory and bite.
- Always ask permission from an animal's owner before approaching their animal—even if you have played with the animal in the past.
- Never approach an animal that appears injured or sick.
- Never approach stray animals.
- Tell an adult about a stray animal.

For the Adults:

- Contact your local animal shelter or animal control office first to give a good description of the animal. This gives them a chance to match the found animal in case the owner contacts the shelter.

- If you decide to try to find the owner yourself, contact your local animal shelter and provide a description of the animal you've found. This gives the opportunity for the agency to reunite the animal with the owners.

- Have the animal scanned for a microchip. This ID check may help you find the owner more quickly.

- Create a "found pet" poster to post in the area where the animal was found.

- Drive your area and look for "lost pet" posters to see if they match the animal you found.
- Research Social Media sites for found and lost pet pages. Many cities and rescue groups have started using popular social media sites to spread the word quickly when pets are lost and found.
- You can also post notices at veterinary hospitals and on websites such as www.Petfinder.com.
- If you decide to house the animal until it is found, please follow these precautions. If you have other pets at home, make sure you can keep them separate from the found animal until you can make sure the animal isn't sick or aggressive with other animals.
- If you can't provide shelter for the animal, arrange to have the animal

picked up by an agency as soon as possible.

- If you've tried to find the owner without success, but are unable to keep the animal long-term, you can try to find it a new home.

Are You a Rescuer At Heart?

If you know you have the heart of a rescuer, then equip yourself to do the best job possible.

Provided below is a checklist of some items to keep in your car at all times:

- Your Phone
- Phone numbers of a local animal control, a shelter, and a 24-hour emergency veterinary clinic
- Cat carrier or cardboard box

- A collapsible wire dog kennel
- Collars, or harnesses, and a few strong leashes for dogs. Determine what size dogs you feel comfortable rescuing and make the necessary preparations.
- Heavy blanket
- Water bowls and water
- Strong-smelling foods, such as canned tuna or dried liver
- An animal emergency first-aid kit

Denver's Activity Pages

Connect the dots to find Denver's favorite squeaky toy. Lady says it no longer has it's squeak. Guess who broke the squeaker? _ _ _ _ _ _ _

Denver's favorite things about his playtime are chasing toys, searching for leaves and sniffing for raccoons. What do you like to do when you play?
Write them down below or draw a little picture on the next page.

1. _____

_____

2. _____

_____

3. _____

_____

Coloring Pages

Think about it..

1. How do you think Denver felt when he saw the car drive away?

2. How would you feel if that happened to you?

3. Have you ever felt that way?

4. How does your face look when you feel that way?

5. Which parts of Denver's story did you like?

6. What parts of Denver's story would you change?

7. How do you think Denver felt when he knew he had a new family?

Do you like jokes?

Here is sample from Denver's "Live. Love. Laugh: Paws and Tails Joke Book" coming soon!

Find out more at www.DenverTheDog.com

Why was the dog stealing shingles?

Because he wanted to be a WOOFER!

What happened when the dog went to the flea circus?

He stole the show!

What happens when it rains cats and dogs?

You step in a POODLE!

ABOUT THE AUTHOR

As a child, Kim Steadman grew up in a quiet suburb outside of Dallas, TX. You would never know she was so near to the city. Her childhood homes nestled near wooded areas or expanses of fields. While she loved her friends, her greatest friends were her books.

When she was a little girl, she used to play library with her dolls. Her shelf of books in her bedroom served as the library. Each doll borrowed a book to read. She would spend her time reading to them and explored the fantastical world of reading.

Her favorite story books always had main characters with animals and mythical creatures. It was through books she developed a lifelong love of furry and winged creatures. She's rescued everything from birds, cats, raccoons, and, yes, dogs.

She and her husband now live near one of her childhood homes. Their two fur-children, Zak (Grumpy Dog) and Denver, the Recycled Dog run the show. You can read more about her at www.KimSteadman.com

There are other dogs like Denver and they all deserve a second chance. Dogs aren't meant to be thrown away like garbage.

If your family decides to add a furry member, consider adopting from your local animal shelter or fostering animals in need of temporary homes.